Bill Could Tell and *Judy Stood Up*– Volumes II & III

Privacy, Due Process of the Law, Voting Corruption and Justice

—by Bill Watkins

Traveling Poet Press – Livingston, Montana 2017

2

Bill loved to play. Sports mostly…

He loved to spend time with his dad, but didn't see him as much as he wanted as his mom and dad were separated.

One day, Bill was at study on a computer in class a couple minutes past the lunch bell, researching more about the United States Constitution.

A friend ran in and reminded Bill about lunch.

Bill powered the computer off, grabbed a sack lunch and followed his friend to the outside lunch area.

P.E. followed lunch, which was Bill's favorite period, unless Coach Saxon was on, who was unpopular with many of the students.

When the kids got their lockers, they were assured of privacy, given locks with combinations only they knew.

Little did Bill and the others know, though:

Coach Saxon had a master key to all the locks, something revealed to the one o'clock P.E. class when the students all saw that their lockers had been raided, their gym clothes and belongings tossed.

BILL COULD TELL something was wrong, then remembered his studies:

"Coach Saxon, you have no right to search through our belongings without probable cause that a crime has been committed."

Saxon was taken aback by the young prodigy's conviction.

Bill began to quote the Fourth Amendment:

The right of the people to be secure in their persons, houses, papers, and effects, against unreasonable searches and seizures, shall not be violated, and no Warrants shall issue, but upon probable cause, supported by Oath or affirmation, and particularly describing the place to be searched, and the persons or things to be seized.

While the students and Coach Saxon marveled, Bill explained himself:

"I Googled it."

Coach Saxon apologized and walked away for a moment.

The kids smiled, laughed and shook Bill's hand.

They had a great game in P.E. that day, and Coach Saxon was nicer than usual.

Judy Stood Up – Volume II

Due Process of the Law

8

It wasn't long before Judy heard about Bill's exploits in the gym.

When she and Bill met for their weekly policy discussions, she brought up other Constitutional amendments of interest.

"What about the fifth, sixth and fourteenth amendments, Bill?"

Bill just sat back and listened.

What interested Judy so much was the way the U.S. Constitution was amended to secure the rights even of those accused of committing crimes.

Both these students were concerned in Social Studies one day, when they learned a history book said Lee Harvey Oswald killed someone without a court ruling.

"There was no defense offered the accused!!" Judy blurted out to their teacher's dismay.

The teacher had no good answer for why Oswald or anyone else worldwide gets a label attached to them as "criminal" without "due process of the law."

Now: "due process of the law" could just be called a "fair shot" where the person deciding if someone was guilty gets to see two sides of the story.

Bill came over to Judy's house one day, and they were watching the news.

There was talk of an "air raid on terrorists" and later of such and such president gassing his own people.

In both cases, there was no legal process; just the news saying something, bombers killing, and politicians assuring us "they got the bad guys."

Judy was almost in tears, thinking of how corrupt our country can be, law-wise.

She showed Bill her highlighted U.S. Constitution and its Bill of Rights:

"...nor be deprived of life, liberty, or property, without due process of law" stood out to Bill, along with *"the accused shall enjoy the right to a speedy and public trial, by an impartial jury of the State,"* then seeing more about *"right to counsel"* and defense.

"Why can't adults follow our Constitution?" Judy probed.

Bill just pondered Judy's question, added some notes to her highlights and shook his head.

JUDY STOOD UP, shook off her frustration, and began to draft a letter to her local Congressman.

Bill Could Tell – Volume III

Voting Corruption

Bill was sick of money winning political seats instead of ideas.

"I mean," he complained to Judy, "First they keep *us* out illegally"—

"Discrimination!!" Judy interrupted loudly.

Nodding, Bill continued: "Dang right!!! Then all kinds of other people and their ideas cannot be heard because of all the money adults put into a political campaign.

"Yeah," Judy responded. "What do lawn signs and posters have to do with better sidewalks and roads?"

"Or better police?" Chimed Robert, a latecomer to the meeting.

Bill and Judy had been trying to recruit people to their weekly political meetings, but had after two months found only Robert from the fourth grade to join.

"I'm so sick of the corruption. The age discrimination. Money over Ideas!!" exclaimed an exasperated Bill.

That was before another new recruit arrived.

His name was Deep Horse, and he had the farthest trip to make to get to school everyday.

"Money, metal and concrete over our land!" Deep Horse added, and the four huddled to take notes, look things up on the school computer, and talk.

BILL COULD TELL that Deep Horse would add a lot to their conversations, as he was Native American.

"You can't get more American than Deep Horse!!" Bill bragged to Judy on his way home from the meeting at school.

"We are lucky to have him in our group, to be sure," Judy agreed.

"Now, how do we get adults to look down and hear us?" Bill posed.

"We'll ask Deep Horse tomorrow."

They both thought that wise, and it is wise to listen to Native Americans about this land they were one with for years and years before the European migration to the United States.

18

Judy Stood Up – Volume III

Justice

"We can't vote because they discriminate. You can't even run for Congress until you are twenty-five years old!!" whined Judy in their weekly political discussion.

"Thirty for the Senate, thirty-five to run for the presidency!" added Bill, as Robert and Deep Horse listened.

For weeks, Judy and Bill marveled at how quiet Deep Horse was. Then all of a sudden, he would stand up and make a short, perfect, wise speech.

"It seems like he is praying while he speaks," Robert once noticed while walking home with Judy.

"Yes," Judy agreed.

Judy liked Robert, whose own background was different than hers. Robert said his parents were from Mexico, and he spoke Spanish as well as English!

Someone would call her interest in Robert a romantic one if they could know her thoughts. Both Robert and Judy liked being with each other, but had not said words about their feelings.

"See you tomorrow," Judy said as Robert walked into his house.

Instead of being sad he did not express his feelings, Robert chased Judy down a couple steps and gave her a kiss on the cheek.

Judy blushed and walked away with a jump in her step; Robert the same.

The next meeting of the junior political group saw a fifth member, an African American fifth grader named Veronica.

She came with research already done on the twenty-sixth amendment:

The right of citizens of the United States, who are <u>eighteen years of age or</u>

older, to vote, shall not be denied or abridged by the United States or any state on account of age.

The group all shook their heads at the insanity, pulled out their new text books, *The Notvarov Chronicles*, about a children's revolt and surge for the vote.

JUDY STOOD UP, looked to Deep Horse, and asked him to comment.

Deep horse sat. Breathed. Seemed to pray a moment upward, then stood next to Judy before she sat.

"I have always been troubled by the American government. The trouble was explained to me by my parents, who were told by their parents. I think if the problems can be summed up, it would be that many people who have come to this land have a disease of 'more,' and they are never satisfied with what they have. They keep taking, but are never full or happy."

Deep Horse stopped, gave way as the newcomer Veronica patted him on the back, took over the floor:

"Deep Horse is right. The problems of today come from the problems of the past, many of which have not been solved."

"Slavery was wrong!" Robert offered.

"And yet no reparations have been made to make up for the sins of slavery," added Bill.

"Let us make a new political party," Judy offered.

"A Native Party," agreed Robert, and all shook hands and high-fived, preparing to write their congressmen, engage and change the world.

Love,

Coach Waffle

www.ingramcontent.com/pod-product-compliance
Lightning Source LLC
Chambersburg PA
CBHW041121180526
45172CB00001B/363